Original title:
The Glow of the Woods

Author: Sabrina Sarvik
ISBN HARDBACK: 978-9908-1-1417-0
ISBN PAPERBACK: 978-9908-1-1418-7
ISBN EBOOK: 978-9908-1-1419-4

Interwoven Moments of Twinkling Glimpses

In the air, a melody plays,
Laughter dances in sunlit rays.
Colorful lights twinkling bright,
Hearts sing together, pure delight.

Banners flutter in the gentle breeze,
Whispers of joy, among the trees.
Tables laden with treats to share,
Love woven tightly, everywhere.

Sparkling eyes, a shared embrace,
Memories linger in every space.
Fireworks light the velvet sky,
Dreams take flight, soaring high.

As evening falls, the stars align,
Together we bask, in moments divine.
Cheers and toasts, the night ignites,
With joy that sparkles, our hearts take flight.

Whispers of Light in the Canopy

Beneath the bright and swirling leaves,
Dancing shadows gently weave.
Laughter spills in golden streams,
Whispers float like faded dreams.

Sunbeams break through the emerald pride,
Where joy and secrets often hide.
A celebration fills the air,
Nature's song beyond compare.

Radiance Beneath the Boughs

In the twilight's tender grace,
Brightened hearts begin to race.
Every leaf a sparkling gem,
Enchantment whispers, time to stem.

Gather close, the night unfolds,
Sharing warmth as the tale is told.
With every cheer, the stars align,
In this realm, the stars do shine.

Glimmering Secrets of the Forest

Moonlit paths where creatures play,
Laughter echoes, come what may.
In the glimmers soft and bright,
Magic stirs within the night.

In the canopy, colors blend,
Joyous spirits, hearts extend.
Underneath the whispered tune,
The forest glows, a festive boon.

Shadows Need No Flame

Dancing lightly on the ground,
Laughter's joy is all around.
In the dusk where dreams collide,
Shadows twirl, and hearts abide.

No need for light where glee ignites,
Magic lives in starry nights.
Every step, a song anew,
In the shadows, joy breaks through.

Sunlight's Kiss on the Woodland Floor

Beneath the trees, the light cascades,
A dance of warmth, in sunlit glades.
Each leaf a star, a shimmering gold,
Whispers of stories, waiting to be told.

The flowers bloom in vibrant cheer,
With laughter carried on the breeze near.
Nature's palette, so bold and bright,
Welcomes all with pure delight.

Flickering Joy in Sylvan Shadows

In glades where secrets softly roam,
Joy flickers like fireflies, far from home.
Crickets sing a merry tune,
As dusk unveils a silver moon.

Branches sway with playful grace,
A gentle waltz, a warm embrace.
In the hush, the heart takes flight,
Painting dreams in the fading light.

Hallowed Glow of Nature’s Embrace

A hallowed glow, the forest sighs,
As twilight wraps the earth in ties.
The air is sweet with woodsy scent,
In every corner, joy is lent.

The brook's soft murmur sings of peace,
In nature's arms, all troubles cease.
With every leaf, a tale unfolds,
In whispers soft, like tales of old.

Radiant Hues in the Heart of Green

Amidst the green, a vibrant song,
Where colors blend, we all belong.
Petals burst in shades so bright,
A symphony of pure delight.

The sunlight dances on the stream,
In nature’s world, we often dream.
Every step a joyous beat,
In the heart of green, life feels complete.

Rays of Joy Amidst Woven Boughs

Beneath the sunlit canopy bright,
Laughter weaves through branches light.
Children dance on carpets green,
Joy unfolds in every scene.

Colorful banners flutter high,
Whispers of secrets in the sky.
Every smile a cherished song,
Together where we all belong.

Ephemeral Glows Along Forest Paths

Twinkling lights like fireflies,
Guide our steps beneath the skies.
Every turn a tale to tell,
In this vibrant, magic spell.

Crisp air filled with scents so sweet,
Nature’s rhythm, skip our beat.
Hand in hand, we wander free,
In the heart of festivity.

The Enchantment of Luminescent Flora

Petals glow in twilight's grace,
Each adorned in nature's lace.
Bells of laughter, soft and clear,
Echo joy for all to hear.

Moonlight dances on the stream,
Creating shapes that make us dream.
Every star a friend so dear,
Binding us in warmth and cheer.

Celestial Whispers in Canopy Courts

Underneath the giant trees,
Voices mingle with the breeze.
Echoes of love fill the air,
As we gather, hearts laid bare.

Glimmers shine on paths we walk,
Each sweet moment, laughter talks.
In this court of sky and ground,
Festive joy forever found.

Reflections of the Sun's Gentle Hand

Golden rays dance on the stream,
A warm embrace, a glowing dream.
Laughter echoes, joy is spun,
In the sparkle of the sun.

Children's giggles fill the air,
Blossoms painted with bright flair.
Every heart beats in delight,
Underneath the morning light.

Shadows play upon the ground,
As summer's whispers swirl around.
Nature's canvas, vibrant and grand,
All aglow from the sun's kind hand.

With each moment, life’s parade,
In this festive sunlit glade.
Let’s dance beneath the azure sky,
As day rolls on, let spirits fly.

Nature's Fireflies in Whispered Breeze

In the twilight, fireflies spark,
Dancing slowly, lighting the dark.
Whispers float on a gentle sigh,
As the stars emerge in the sky.

Fields of gold beneath the night,
Nature’s heartbeat, soft and bright.
A symphony of crickets' tune,
Guides the way to the silver moon.

Children chase these glowing beads,
Collecting dreams among the reeds.
Every flicker tells a tale,
Of summer nights, where spirits sail.

With the breeze, we laugh and twirl,
As magic dances, hearts unfurl.
In this gathering, pure as air,
We find the joy we love to share.

The Dream of Sunlit Ferns

Amidst the woods, where shadows play,
Sunlit ferns sway in joyous array.
Nature's fingers gently trace,
The beauty of this secret place.

Breezes whisper through the trees,
As laughter carries on the breeze.
Where colors merge in vibrant schemes,
We wander deep in nature's dreams.

The warmth of sunlight, soft and bright,
Holds every heart in pure delight.
In the rustle of leaves, we find,
The treasures of the heart and mind.

Let's celebrate, as seasons blend,
With every step, the joys extend.
In harmony, together we sway,
In this sunlit dance, come what may.

Ethereal Light Beneath the Branches

In the forest, shadows weave,
Golden glimmers, we believe.
Branches arch like open arms,
Drawing hearts with day’s sweet charms.

The air is filled with laughter’s song,
As nature hums, we all belong.
In every sunbeam, stories flow,
Of hidden paths where wise ones go.

Mossy carpets cradle our feet,
Every moment feels complete.
Underneath the canopy wide,
We share our hopes with joy and pride.

As twilight descends with grace,
We gather close in this sacred space.
With hearts aglow and spirits high,
Underneath the stars, let’s fly.

Mystique of the Illuminated Canopy

Under a sky of twinkling stars,
Laughter echoes from afar.
Branches dance with lights so bright,
Whispers weave through the night.

Beneath the glow of lanterns high,
Dreams take flight, spirits sigh.
Colors shimmer, shadows play,
Magic lingers, hearts sway.

Luminous Secrets of the Verdant Realm

In the glade where fireflies gleam,
Nature sings a vibrant theme.
Petals blush in softest light,
Joy abounds in pure delight.

The air is sweet with fragrant blooms,
As laughter fills the garden rooms.
Every leaf, a whispered tale,
Festive hearts begin to sail.

Dappled Light on Earthly Pages

Sunlight dapples through the trees,
Carrying whispers on the breeze.
Books of joy unfold their rhyme,
Each page turned, a moment in time.

Gathered friends with smiles aglow,
Stories shared both fast and slow.
The world alight with hope and cheer,
Moments cherished, staying near.

Soft Hues in the Forest's Embrace

Gentle hues of green and gold,
Joyous secrets to behold.
Songs of birds in harmony,
Nature's dance, our symphony.

Warmth of sun on every face,
Hearts entwined in sweet embrace.
The forest whispers in delight,
A festive promise, pure and bright.

Sunbeams Weaving Stories in Bark

Golden rays dance lightly,
Caressing the aged tree,
Whispers of laughter echo,
In the breeze, wild and free.

Children gather in circles,
Painting dreams in the air,
With every giggle and shout,
Joy flows everywhere.

Nature’s canvas comes alive,
Where sunlight guides our play,
Each branch tells a tale anew,
In this warm, bright ballet.

Sunbeams weave through the forest,
In a tapestry so bright,
Every corner bursts with life,
In this magical light.

Flickers of Hope in the Quiet Grove

Softly glows the twilight,
As shadows stretch and blend,
Crickets serenade us quietly,
With nature as our friend.

Beneath the spreading branches,
Stars begin to peek through,
Each flicker shares a secret,
Of dreams we wish to pursue.

Laughter floats like petals,
On the gentle evening air,
In the grove, we share wishes,
And hopes beyond compare.

Every sigh is a promise,
As the moon begins to rise,
Uniting hearts in silence,
Under luminous skies.

The Secret Language of Swaying Leaves

Leaves whisper tales of summer,
In a language soft and sweet,
Fluttering in the warm wind,
With every rustling beat.

They dance with joyful secrets,
A rhythm only they know,
Telling stories of the sun,
And the moon's gentle glow.

In their sway, we find comfort,
As they shimmy through the air,
With every laugh and chatter,
They invite us to this fair.

Beneath the leafy canopy,
Together, in delight,
We join the leaves in laughter,
Celebrating the night.

Radiant Whispers Beneath the Stars

Under a quilt of twinkling lights,
We gather, blissfully near,
With every flicker and shimmer,
Our hearts beat loud and clear.

Stories shared like constellations,
In the cozy night embrace,
Each point of light a moment,
We hold in this sacred space.

The laughter spills like starlight,
Echoing into the dark,
United by our wishes,
We ignite the glowing spark.

As the night wraps around us,
With magic in the air,
We dance beneath the cosmos,
Our joys beyond compare.

Ethereal Beams Through Ancient Trees

Golden light filters through the leaves,
Whispering secrets only the forest believes.
Dancing shadows on the mossy ground,
Nature's chorus, a harmonious sound.

Branches sway, cradling the sun,
A symphony of life, bright and fun.
Birds sing sweetly, a jubilant tune,
Under the gaze of the radiant moon.

The Luminescent Heart of Ferns

Emerald fronds in soft, gentle glow,
Cradling dreams that mysteries sow.
Each droplet sparkles like a star,
In the stillness, magic travels far.

Beneath cool canopies, spirits rise,
In the tender dance where silence lies.
A festival of life, vivid and bright,
In the heart of fern, pure delight.

Moonlit Murmurs in the Underbrush

The night whispers secrets, mysterious and deep,
While shadows dance lightly, in slumber they sweep.
Crickets serenade in the cool evening air,
As fireflies twinkle, shining everywhere.

Rustling leaves tell tales of joy alive,
In the underbrush, where the wild things thrive.
A celebration of life, so vivid, so grand,
Guided by the light of the moon’s gentle hand.

Dawn's Embrace in Sylvan Corners

The sun peeks softly through branches entwined,
Her warm golden arms, gently refined.
Awakening blossoms, a colorful spree,
In the embrace of dawn, all spirits are free.

Birds chirp bright greetings, a welcoming song,
In the soft morning light, where we all belong.
Festive joy swells in the freshness of day,
Where nature unveils her enchanting display.

Ethereal Essence of Rooted Giants

Tall trees sway in the gentle breeze,
Whispers of secrets, carried with ease.
Branches adorned with life’s vibrant glow,
Nature's dance puts on an enchanting show.

Luminous lights through canopies peep,
Awake from slumber, where shadows leap.
Mirth in the air, laughter takes flight,
Celebration blooms in the soft fading light.

Hearts align with the rhythm of roots,
In harmony wrapped, where joy bears fruits.
Rooted giants bask in their grace,
Festive spirits join in this celestial space.

Veils of Mystery in the Twilit Glade

Veils of fog drift with a playful tease,
Mysterious whispers float through the trees.
Moonbeams sprinkle silver upon the ground,
In twilit glades, where wonders abound.

Echoes of laughter from faraway lands,
Hand in hand, we weave together our plans.
Every heartbeat resonates with the night,
In splendor and bliss, our dreams take flight.

Pixies appear in a merry parade,
Dancing through shadows that sweetly cascade.
An effervescent charm in the air,
As festive delights unravel with flair.

Glistening Moments on Forest Floors

Glistening dewdrops like gems lay in wait,
Awakening morning, an ethereal state.
Sunlight cascades on the mossy bed,
Warmth embraces, as night softly fled.

With each gentle step, leaves whisper a tune,
Forest alive beneath the brightening moon.
Gathered together, friends take a stand,
In harmonious rhythm, their joys are unplanned.

Laughter erupts, spilling into the air,
Merriment lingers, it dances everywhere.
With hearts intertwined, our spirits explore,
Every moment cherished, forever adored.

Twilight’s Caress on Feathered Ferns

In twilight's embrace, where the cool winds sigh,
Feathered ferns glisten beneath the soft sky.
Each leaf a canvas, painted with dreams,
Awash in colors, where magic redeems.

Gathered around, storytelling unfolds,
Whispers of blessings, in twilight retold.
Cascading laughter envelops the glade,
A festive celebration, never to fade.

With drums in the distance, the night brings delight,
Echoes of joy fill the deepening night.
In a circle of warmth, our spirits unite,
Together we dance in the soft fading light.

Embedded Light in Nature's Tapestry

The sun breaks through the leafy maze,
Dancing beams in golden rays.
Flowers bloom with colors bright,
Nature hums in pure delight.

Birds chirp tunes of joyous flight,
Gentle breezes take their height.
Streams reflect a twinkling gleam,
All alive in vibrant dream.

Nature's Hidden Flickers of Warmth

In the forest's dappled glow,
Hidden magic starts to flow.
Branches sway with whispers sweet,
Life unfolds where shadows meet.

Mossy carpets cushion feet,
Nature's pulse is soft and fleet.
Crickets sing their lullabies,
Underneath the starlit skies.

Soft Illumination of Somnolent Leaves

Leaves aglow with twilight's kiss,
Wrapped in nature's soothing bliss.
Glistening under silver light,
Resting softly through the night.

Moonbeams weave through branches thin,
Cradling dreams as day grows dim.
In this hush, hearts gently sway,
Underneath the Milky Way.

Glints of Magic in Winding Routes

Paths adorned with shimmering dreams,
Nature sparkles in silver beams.
Whispers echo down the way,
Guiding souls at break of day.

Every turn a tale unfolds,
In the breeze, a warmth that holds.
Steps taken with a sense of glee,
In this land of revelry.

Luminous Trails Through Leafy Halls

In leafy halls where lanterns glow,
Shadows dance with a soft, warm flow.
Joyous laughter fills the air,
As vibrant colors swirl with flair.

Pumpkin pies and cider sweet,
Gather 'round for a festive treat.
Songs of cheer, both near and far,
Underneath the twinkling stars.

Friends entwined in warmth and glee,
Celebrate with hearts so free.
Each moment cherished, spirits bright,
In this hall of pure delight.

Enchanted Gleams of Twilight

As twilight paints the sky with grace,
Glimmers dance in a soft embrace.
Whispers of magic fill the night,
Underneath the stars so bright.

Candles flicker, shadows play,
Songs of joy drift away.
With every step, a spark of cheer,
Echoes of laughter fill the sphere.

Balloons float with colors bold,
Stories shared, both new and old.
In this twilight, hearts unite,
In the magic of moonlight.

Beyond the Mossy Path

Beyond the path where moss does grow,
Festive whispers begin to flow.
Lights like fireflies twinkle bright,
Guiding hearts through the special night.

Dancing flowers sway with glee,
Nature's song in harmony.
With every step, a beat so sweet,
Celebrate where life and joy meet.

Gathered friends, hand in hand,
In this enchanted, dream-like land.
With soft laughter, love’s soft call,
Together, we embrace it all.

Celestial Dances Among the Pines

Beneath the pines, where starlight falls,
We celebrate, our spirit calls.
Celestial dances paint the night,
Magic glows with a pure delight.

Fires crackle, stories unfold,
Of adventures, brave and bold.
Laughter echoes, warm and bright,
In the heart of this sacred light.

Sparkling stars share their glow,
In this gathering, love will flow.
Join the dance, let spirits soar,
In this festive forevermore.

The Gentle Flicker of Fairy Dances

In twilight's glow, soft whispers hum,
Tiny lights flicker, a joyous drum.
Around the glade, laughter takes flight,
Fairies twirl, weaving dreams in the night.

Beneath the stars, their sparkles play,
Guiding lost hearts along the way.
With every twirl, a wish is spun,
In enchanted circles, all is won.

The nightingale sings, a melody sweet,
Where dreams and wonder softly meet.
Each fluttering wing, a tale to tell,
In this magical realm, all is well.

So dance, oh fairies, under soft moonlight,
In gentle whispers, pure and bright.
For in your movements, joy is found,
In the gentle flicker, love abounds.

Murmurs of Light in Forest's Breath

The forest stirs with glimmers bright,
Moonbeams weave through leafy height.
Nature's whispers, a soft embrace,
Invite all souls to find their place.

Among the trunks, the shadows play,
Laughter mingles with night’s ballet.
Each pulse of warmth, a shared delight,
Murmurs of light, guiding the night.

Crickets serenade with rhythms clear,
In the heart of woods, peace draws near.
Where glistening paths unfold with grace,
Every soul finds their sacred space.

So wander deep where the wild things sing,
Embrace the joy that the forest brings.
With every step, let your worries cease,
In murmured light, discover peace.

Rays of Hope Through Elder Trees

Golden rays filter through ancient boughs,
Whispers of sunshine, nature's vows.
Each leaf glistens with hope anew,
In the heart of woods, dreams come true.

The elder trees stand tall and wise,
Guardians of secrets beneath the skies.
In their embrace, the world feels bright,
Radiating love, casting pure light.

Soft breezes carry laughter around,
Filling the air with a joyful sound.
Every flower blooms with radiant hue,
Dancing in rhythm, a vibrant view.

So linger here, let worries fade,
In this haven, be unafraid.
For in these woods, hope always glees,
Beneath the rays of elder trees.

The Radiant Secret of Sylvan Souls

In a hidden grove, where shadows rest,
Sylvan souls gather, truly blessed.
With sparkling eyes and hearts aglow,
They share their secrets, soft and slow.

The crystal streams sing lulling tunes,
To the rhythm of light beneath the moons.
Laughter flows like water, pure,
In this radiant space, hearts find cure.

Threads of magic weave through the air,
Binding the souls with love and care.
Each joyous moment, a treasure to hold,
In tales of wonder, softly told.

So join the dance in nature's embrace,
With sylvan souls, find your place.
For in this radiant secret, delight,
Awaits the heart in the stillness of night.

Light's Dance Through Verdant Veils

In the glade where sunlight streams,
Colors twirl in joyful gleams.
Leaves and shadows intertwine,
Nature's stage, a grand design.

Laughter echoes through the trees,
Carried gently by the breeze.
Children play with hearts so light,
Chasing beams that fade from sight.

Golden rays in soft embrace,
Whisper secrets, time and space.
Happiness in every glance,
Underneath the light's bright dance.

As dusk draws near with velvet skies,
Fireflies flicker, magic flies.
In this realm, the spirit sings,
Of the joy that nature brings.

Echoes of Illumination Beneath Canopies

Beneath the boughs, a world aglow,
Painting dreams where soft winds blow.
Whispers sweet that fill the air,
Nature's song beyond compare.

Lanterns bright in every hue,
Guide the wanderers, old and new.
Moments linger, joy unfurl,
As laughter swirls in playful whirl.

Every glance, a spark ignites,
In the harmony of lights.
Underneath the whispered trees,
We find solace, we find ease.

A tapestry of night unfolds,
Every story sweetly told.
Beneath the stars’ enchanting sway,
We dance through life, we laugh and play.

Radiance of the Forest's Heart

In the heart where flora thrives,
Healing light in nature drives.
Every bloom a fragrant song,
In the forest where we belong.

Glimmers spark on lively streams,
Awakening our sweetest dreams.
Rustling leaves bring tales of yore,
Amidst the woods, we long for more.

Sunbeams peek through emerald crew,
Kindling joy in every view.
The forest breathes, a vibrant art,
Wrapped in warmth, a joyful heart.

As shadows blend with light's embrace,
Each moment glows with sweet grace.
In this haven, peace imparts,
The radiance of nature’s heart.

Twilight's Embrace in the Thicket

As daylight fades, the magic stirs,
Beneath the trees, a world of furs.
Shadows lengthen, colors blend,
In twilight’s arms, our hearts transcend.

Firelight dances, a flickering glow,
Stories shared where friendships grow.
Each laugh a note in night’s sweet song,
In this moment, we all belong.

The air is rich with scented pine,
Time slows, serenity divine.
Wrapped in whispers, branches sway,
In twilight's warmth, we softly play.

When stars appear with silver gleam,
We gather close, like a sweet dream.
In every smile, in every glance,
Life’s a festival, a timeless dance.

Salmon Skies and Emerald Shadows

In the blush of dawn's embrace,
Salmon skies ignite the day,
Emerald shadows dance in place,
Nature's hues in bright display.

Joyful laughter fills the air,
Children play beneath the trees,
Every moment free from care,
Whispers carried by the breeze.

Picnics spread on gentle grass,
Sunshine sparkles on the lake,
Time slips by, too swift to pass,
Memories in our hearts we'll make.

Luminous Pathways Through Thorny Thickets

Luminous paths where lanterns glow,
Twinkling lights like stars at night,
Through thorny thickets, spirits flow,
Every corner reveals delight.

Festival of colors bright,
Joy and laughter intertwine,
In the warmth of soft moonlight,
Hearts united, spirits shine.

Dancing figures, shadows play,
Winding trails with music sway,
Echoes of the night’s ballet,
Guiding us in a festive way.

Hold Your Breath in Gentle Glow

Hold your breath in gentle glow,
Fireflies twinkling, nature's art,
Magic weaves, the night is slow,
Every flicker warms the heart.

Elfin whispers in the trees,
Tales of old, enchantments grand,
Softly swaying, sweet as breeze,
Festive spirits hand in hand.

As the starlit canvas spreads,
Hope and wonder intertwine,
In this world where joy embeds,
Every moment feels divine.

Silhouettes Against a Dazzling Backdrop

Silhouettes against the sky,
Dazzling hues of sunset blaze,
Celebrations lift us high,
In the twilight's golden rays.

Drums are beating, feet will dance,
Rhythms echo through the night,
In this vibrant, joyful trance,
Hearts aglow with pure delight.

Every laugh, a shining star,
Stories told by candlelight,
Together here, no place too far,
In this festival of life.

Tales Told by Flickering Light

In the glow of candles bright,
Whispers dance, sparking delight,
Stories weave through starlit night,
Laughter echoes, hearts take flight.

Friends gather 'round with cheerful cheer,
Every tale draws them near,
Joyful memories appear,
In this moment, love is clear.

Colors spin in vibrant hues,
Guided by the softest muse,
Radiant warmth, the soul renews,
As the world begins to fuse.

Underneath the moon's embrace,
Each flicker, we find our place,
In the charm of time and space,
Life’s a dance, a wondrous chase.

Harmony of Shadow and Light's Embrace

As daylight fades, the shadows play,
In twilight's arms, they softly sway,
A symphony of night and day,
In every heart, a song to stay.

The stars emerge, a glowing band,
Twinkling bright, hand in hand,
In this dance, we understand,
How love lives in this wonderland.

Silhouettes of joy take flight,
Painting dreams in the soft night,
Echoes of laughter, pure delight,
Agree to bask in nature's light.

Harmony sings in gentle tones,
Uniting souls, banishing groans,
In shadows cast, our love is sown,
Together forever, never alone.

Luminance in the Forsaken Path

A flicker glows on the narrow trail,
Guiding the lost where shadows prevail,
Hope ignites, we shall not fail,
As night whispers its ancient tale.

Crickets serenade the starlit night,
With every note, the world feels right,
Unity blossoms in sheer delight,
In darkness shines our spirits bright.

Bright lanterns sway, we smile and sing,
Creating warmth, hearts take wing,
In the glow, our dreams take swing,
Together, joy is what we bring.

The path ahead, a vibrant dance,
Each shadow holds a hidden chance,
In luminance, we find romance,
In this life, we take our stance.

The Song of Fireflies in Twilight's Grasp

In twilight's grasp, the fireflies glow,
Dancing beams in a soft, warm flow,
Nature's chorus sings sweet and low,
A celebration, hearts overflow.

They flit about like stars in flight,
Painting dreams in the enveloping night,
Wonders unfold in their gentle light,
Whispers of magic, pure and bright.

Underneath the canopy of trees,
The world resonates with gentle ease,
In this harmony, our minds appease,
Finding joy in nature's decrees.

The song of fireflies brings delight,
As shadows wane, and spirits ignite,
In this moment, everything feels right,
Our hearts alight, a future so bright.

Radiant Mirages in the Underbrush

In the thicket where colors gleam,
Dancing lights weave a radiant dream.
Whispers of joy in daylight's embrace,
Nature’s canvas, a festive space.

With laughter echoing far and wide,
Beneath the leaves, where secrets hide.
Swaying flowers join in the cheer,
With every petal, a wish draws near.

A tapestry bright, woven with care,
The underbrush sings—come and share!
Sparkling moments fill the air,
In this realm, harmony is rare.

Radiant mirages dance in the glow,
A festival born where wild things grow.
As sunlight plays on each vibrant hue,
The underbrush whispers, “Celebrate too!”

Harmony in the Flickering Limelight

Beneath the stars where dreams ignite,
A stage unfolds in the soft moonlight.
With flickering shadows, the dancers sway,
In unison, they greet the night's ballet.

The air is thick with laughter and song,
Each whispered note draws the crowd along.
Colors burst like fireflies bright,
In this lively embrace, hearts take flight.

Echoes of joy in soft murmured tones,
Pulse with the rhythm, like heartbeats, alone.
With every twirl, the world melts away,
In this limelight, we choose to stay.

Harmony weaves through every delight,
A festive scene in the still of the night.
Together we bask, hand in hand,
In flickering dreams, on vibrant land.

Archway of Shadows and Shimmer

Beneath archways where shadows blend,
Glimmers of light seem to transcend.
Each corner holds a delight in store,
Inviting us in, to explore more.

With laughter that spills like sweet champagne,
Echoing joy in a soft refrain.
In this realm where the dark meets bright,
Shimmering hopes dance in the night.

Underneath stars that twinkle and wink,
In the gentle hush, we pause and think.
With every step, our spirits soar,
Through this archway, we yearn for more.

Shadows cradle our whispered dreams,
While luminescence bursts at the seams.
A tapestry woven of night and day,
In shimmer and shade, we find our way.

Celestial Signals in the Quietwood

In the quietwood where secrets play,
Celestial signals light the way.
Starlit paths beckon, calm and clear,
As festive wonders draw us near.

Branches sway with a gentle grace,
Each rustle a whisper, a warm embrace.
Under canopies where dreams take flight,
Magic unfurls in the soft moonlight.

The night hums a sweet lullaby,
As constellations weave stories high.
With every glance, the heart takes wing,
In the quietwood, we joyfully sing.

Celestial signals twinkle in glee,
Uniting our spirits, wild and free.
In the stillness, we find our truth,
A celebratory dance of ageless youth.

Spheres of Light Amidst Ancient Timbers

In twilight's glow the lanterns swing,
Their dance a joy, in hearts they sing.
Old branches arch, in shadows cast,
With laughter rich, we breathe the past.

Beneath the boughs, bright colors spin,
As whispers of joy invite us in.
The stars, like gems, above us gleam,
In every heart, a shared sweet dream.

With every smile, the world ignites,
Each flickering light, a spark that excites.
The night unfolds, an endless sea,
In unity, we find our glee.

As time drifts by, the echoes play,
In ancient woods where spirits sway.
With every heartbeat, the tales renew,
Among these timbers, I dance with you.

Moonlit Revelations in Wooded Retreats

Beneath the moon's soft, shimmering glow,
In whispered secrets, our spirits flow.
The leaves, they shimmer, with a silvery hue,
As laughter dances, in rhythms true.

Old trees stand tall, with stories to share,
Each shadowed path, a dream laid bare.
With friends beside, we gather near,
In this wooden haven, joy is sheer.

The night weaves tales of love and light,
In sparkling eyes, the world feels right.
With every glance, new stories bloom,
As life ignites in this joyful room.

The stars above form a radiant lace,
In this sacred place, we find our grace.
Together we sing, under night's embrace,
In moonlit mysteries, love finds its space.

The Ember's Touch on Leafy Canopies

The fire crackles with warmth and cheer,
In leafy realms, we gather here.
Beneath green canopies, sparks take flight,
As whispers drift soft through the night.

Golden embers dance like fireflies bright,
We share our dreams, in the heart of the night.
With every flicker, a story unfolds,
In nature's bosom, our spirit holds.

The fragrance of wood, a sweet embrace,
Each sip of joy, a treasured taste.
Underneath the stars, we feel alive,
In this woven world, together we thrive.

So let the laughter bubble and rise,
As the moon casts light through the starry skies.
In whispers of night, friendships grow,
In the ember's glow, our spirits flow.

Paths Illuminated by Nature's Hand

The winding trails, in gold and green,
Through sunlit groves, in joy we glean.
Each step a rhythm, in nature’s tune,
As light weaves softly, like a monsoon.

With every petal, with every leaf,
We find the magic in simple belief.
The laughter echoes, through trees so grand,
As unity blooms, hand in hand.

The sunbeams kiss, on faces bright,
In every glance, we share delight.
While breezes carry our joyous calls,
In nature’s heart, our spirit sprawls.

So let us wander, where wonders start,
Following paths, that warm the heart.
With every step, let stories blend,
In nature’s light, our souls transcend.

Glimmering Trails of Nature's Palette

In fields where colors dance in light,
Where flowers bloom, a joyous sight.
The butterflies flit, their wings so bright,
Nature's canvas, pure delight.

The gentle breeze brings laughter near,
A melody only hearts can hear.
Each leaf whispers a tale so dear,
In this place, all worries disappear.

Amidst the trees, a playful show,
With every step, the wonders grow.
The sun's warm glow begins to flow,
In glimmering trails, the joy we sow.

So let us wander, hand in hand,
Through this vibrant, festive land.
With every touch of nature's strand,
We bask in beauty, truly grand.

Secrets Hidden in Sunlit Glades

Sunlit glades, where shadows play,
Whispers of magic in the sway.
Each secret nook, a bright display,
In this haven, let us stay.

The sunlight dapples on the ground,
In every rustle, joy is found.
Nature's laughter is the sound,
In the woods, our hearts are bound.

Colorful blooms and buzzing bees,
A symphony carried by the breeze.
In every corner, life agrees,
In sunlit glades, we find our ease.

With every step, the magic grows,
In hidden paths where wildness flows.
Together, let our laughter glow,
As secrets dance in nature's prose.

Shimmering Orbs of the Woodland Night

Under the starry velvet sky,
Shimmering orbs begin to fly.
Fireflies twinkle, oh so spry,
Guiding dreams as night draws nigh.

Whispers of friends around the fire,
Stories shared of joy and desire.
In the stillness, our hearts conspire,
To celebrate, our spirits higher.

Beneath the moon's soft, silvery gleam,
The woodland night unfolds a dream.
In twinkling light, all worries seem,
To vanish like a gentle stream.

So let us dance in shadows bright,
Embracing all this pure delight.
With shimmering orbs, we take our flight,
In woodland nights, our hearts unite.

Golden Rays and Green Embrace

Golden rays through branches peek,
A warm embrace that nature speaks.
In the woods where sunlight leaks,
Our laughter echoes, joy it seeks.

The vibrant green sways in delight,
In every breeze, our spirits light.
With every step, the world feels right,
In this haven, spirits take flight.

Petals flutter like a song,
In perfect harmony, where we belong.
Nature's beauty, a vibrant throng,
In golden rays, we grow more strong.

Together, let us weave our dreams,
In emerald trees, the sunlight gleams.
In this moment, pure joy beams,
In golden rays, life is as it seems.

Enchanted Radiance of the Glade.

In the heart where laughter grows,
Colorful blooms in radiant rows.
Joyful whispers fill the air,
Delight awakens everywhere.

Chimes of joy ring through the night,
Stars above, a twinkling sight.
Dance of fireflies, soft and bright,
Creating magic, pure delight.

Gather 'round the glowing fire,
As shadows play, our hearts conspire.
With every laugh, the night unfolds,
In this glade, our dreams are told.

Celebrate the moment's cheer,
Embracing love when friends are near.
In enchanted grace, we sway,
In the glade, we'll dance and play.

Whispers of Luminous Leaves

Beneath the canopy so lush,
Gentle breezes weave and rush.
Each leaf glimmers, whispers bright,
Telling tales of pure delight.

Skipping paths of dappled light,
Swaying branches, a lovely sight.
Nature's chorus fills the air,
In this realm, beyond compare.

Gathering in this sacred space,
We share laughter, love, and grace.
Moments treasured, hearts so free,
In luminous leaves, we find glee.

As twilight dances on the green,
A tapestry of joy is seen.
In every whisper, echoes flow,
We celebrate, we laugh, we glow.

Enchanted Groves at Twilight

As twilight casts its gentle glow,
In the grove, the magic flows.
Softly shimmer, stars appear,
Whispers of joy fill the atmosphere.

Among the trees where shadows play,
We gather close at end of day.
Songs of friendship, warmth, and light,
In these groves, our spirits take flight.

Candles flicker, illuminating dreams,
In the glow, we weave our themes.
A tapestry of laughter, cheer,
In enchanted groves, love draws near.

Each moment shared, a treasure to hold,
In stories told, and laughter bold.
Together, we greet the night,
In these enchanted groves, all feels right.

Flickering Shadows Among the Trees

Flickering shadows dance and play,
Among the trees, we find our way.
The moonlight spills, lending its glow,
To secret paths where friendships grow.

Laughter echoes through the night,
As we share stories, hearts take flight.
In the rustling leaves, a happy tune,
Under the watchful eye of the moon.

Gather close as embers spark,
Brightening dreams in the dark.
Smiles exchanged, a festive sight,
In flickering shadows, pure delight.

Magic lingers, weaving tight,
In every moment, hearts ignite.
Together we revel, together we roam,
In these shadows, we feel at home.

A Silken Veil of Evening Glow

Twinkling lights adorn the trees,
Whispers of laughter float on the breeze.
Candles flicker with gentle grace,
As shadows dance in the twilight's embrace.

Songs of joy fill the air tonight,
Under the stars, oh what a sight!
Rose petals drift in the soft glow,
With every heartbeat, the spirits grow.

Laughter spills from the hearts so free,
Embraced by the warmth of company.
Moments cherished, forever to keep,
In this dream, we wander deep.

With every toast, we celebrate,
The love that blooms, oh isn't it great?
A silken veil, the evening's song,
In this world, we all belong.

Golden Hues Among the Green

Fields of gold under azure skies,
Nature's canvas, a feast for the eyes.
Sunlight cascades in joyous beams,
Whispering secrets through leafy dreams.

Laughter echoes, children at play,
Chasing shadows both bright and gay.
Amidst the blossoms, butterflies dance,
In this lively and festive romance.

Picnics laid on the soft, warm grass,
As moments of wonder gladly amass.
Every smile shines like the sun,
Together we play, together we run.

Golden hues paint the world around,
Harmony in every joyful sound.
A tapestry woven with laughter and cheer,
In the embrace of this season, we're near.

The Subtle Smile of Sun-Kissed Woods

Amidst the trees, where whispers dwell,
Nature's laughter casts a spell.
Sunlight dances on leaves so green,
In the quiet woods, joy feels unseen.

A brook sings softly, glistening bright,
As shadows stretch to welcome the light.
Footsteps echo on mossy trails,
Where every breeze tells magical tales.

Gathered around in a circle tight,
Stories shared under soft moonlight.
With each heartbeat, the night takes flight,
In the woods, everything feels right.

The subtle smile, the woodland's grace,
Fills our hearts in this sacred space.
A moment to cherish, simple and sweet,
In nature's arms, our souls meet.

Fables Woven with Luminous Threads

Once upon a time in twilight's glow,
Where fables flourish, stories flow.
Luminous threads intertwine with dreams,
In the heart of night, magic redeems.

The moonlight weaves tales of old,
Of heroes brave and treasures untold.
With every turn of the whispered breeze,
Hearts take flight, their worries at ease.

Dancing shadows in the glowing light,
Fables whisper softly to the night.
In every corner, enchantments rise,
Inviting wonder, a sweet surprise.

Gathered together, hand in hand,
Creating moments, so grand, so planned.
With laughter and love, our spirits are fed,
In fables woven with luminous threads.

Phosphorescent Dreams Beneath Tall Pines

Beneath the tall and lofty pines,
Whispers of dreams glow in the night.
Fireflies dance with twinkling signs,
A symphony of joy taking flight.

Laughter echoes through the trees,
Children twirl in merry delight.
Nature hums soft melodies,
Creating magic in the moonlight.

Shadows play on the forest floor,
As lanterns sway in gentle breeze.
Every heart feels forevermore,
In this realm where time's at ease.

Together we sing, under the stars,
As phosphorescent dreams unfold.
In this wondrous place, we'll travel far,
A night of beauty to behold.

Illuminated Memories of Twilit Wanderings

In twilight's glow, we find our way,
Hand in hand through fields of gold.
Whispers of summer in the sway,
Illuminated tales of old.

The firelight dances on our smiles,
While shadows weave their playful part.
We journey softly through the miles,
With every step a spark of heart.

Mellow tunes drift through the trees,
As memories twinkle in the air.
Joy surrounds like a gentle breeze,
Beyond the horizon, dreams laid bare.

We gather ’round as stories flow,
In this festive glow, we are free.
Illuminated moments, bright and slow,
Forever cherished, you and me.

Nature's Canvas in Glowing Hues

Brushstrokes of green beneath the sky,
Nature's art, vibrant and bright.
Petals blooming, oh so spry,
Colors dance in joyous light.

The chorus of leaves, fresh and sweet,
Harmony sings in radiant tones.
Every step a heartbeat's beat,
As laughter mingles with nature's moans.

Brush the canvas where we play,
With skimming glances of the sun.
Life’s a feast on this bright day,
Together, our hearts become one.

In this festival of sights and sounds,
Every moment a radiant view.
With each breath, our love abounds,
In nature’s canvas of glowing hues.

Starlight Filtering Through Mossy Canopies

Under the mossy, verdant embrace,
Starlight dances, soft and pure.
In nature's cradle, we find our place,
A moment that feels secure.

The night unfolds like a tale untold,
Whispers linger among the leaves.
Secrets of heartbeats, vibrant and bold,
A tapestry spun that never leaves.

With every rustle, the night ignites,
Awakening joy from deep within.
In starlit dreams, our spirit ignites,
As nature's magic begins to spin.

Together we weave, beneath the skies,
In this sanctuary, love and cheer.
Starlight filtering, as hope replies,
In our hearts, all is bright and clear.

Shimmering Echoes of Nature’s Breath

In the dawn's embrace, whispers unite,
Colors dance gently, pure delight.
Each leaf’s shimmer sings a bright tune,
Nature’s breath sways beneath the moon.

Laughter of streams in joyous spree,
A symphony woven from land and tree.
Petals unfurl in a fragrant array,
While sunbeams twirl, inviting the day.

Butterflies flutter, their wings a ballet,
As flowers bloom in a vibrant display.
Echoes of joy fill the air so warm,
In shimmering light, love's gentle charm.

Together we bask in this radiant feast,
Nature’s embrace, our hearts find peace.
In every moment, bliss takes its flight,
Shimmering echoes, pure and bright.

Flickering Dreams in the Thicket

Through tangled branches, dreams take flight,
Flickering softly in the warm twilight.
Each shadow whispers secrets untold,
In flickering light, magic unfolds.

Fireflies twinkle, a dance in the dark,
Guiding our hearts with their glimmering spark.
The rustle of leaves composes a tune,
As night blooms beneath a silvered moon.

Children's laughter blends with the night,
Each giggle a wish, a pure delight.
Dreams flicker like stars, alive in our eyes,
In the thicket's embrace, our spirits rise.

Embrace the wonder, let imagination soar,
In this enchanted realm, there’s always more.
Flickering dreams, a heartfelt embrace,
In the thicket's magic, we find our place.

Light’s Serenade Among Stalwart Oaks

Beneath old oaks, where the sunlight plays,
Light’s serenade hums in gentle ways.
Shadows stretch long, as the day unfolds,
In golden hues, every moment holds.

Leaves whisper stories of ages past,
In this sacred space, memories last.
Sunbeams frolic on each sturdy trunk,
A canvas of joy, where hearts are sunk.

Birds in chorus greet the dawn’s rise,
Their melodies dance like twinkling skies.
Glistening dewdrops on emerald blades,
In nature’s embrace, all worries fade.

Together we gather, sharing our cheer,
Under the oaks, we draw all near.
Light’s serenade in our laughter does flow,
A testament that joy always grows.

Beneath the Veil of Verdant Canopy

Beneath the cloak of emerald green,
Magic unfolds in a tranquil scene.
Birdsong lingers in the soft air,
As nature beckons us to share.

Sunlight dapples on the forest floor,
Inviting our hearts to explore.
A breeze carries laughter, sweet and light,
In this hidden realm, our souls take flight.

Each step a whisper, a serene rhyme,
Embraced by nature, lost in time.
We dance through ferns as shadows entwine,
In this verdant world, everything's divine.

Together we hum with the rustling leaves,
Bathed in wonder, our spirit believes.
Beneath the veil, we find our way,
In nature's embrace, forever we stay.

www.ingramcontent.com/pod-product-compliance
Ingram Content Group UK Ltd.
Pitfield, Milton Keynes, MK11 3LW, UK
UKHW030902221224
452712UK00007B/990

9 789908 114170